Colorado

a photographic journey

photography by Blaine Harrington III and Laurence Parent

To my wife, Maureen, who has generously given me the freedom to travel the world for my work during our 29 years together.
—Blaine Harrington III

This book is dedicated to my wife, Patricia, and children, Jason and Michelle, who have accompanied me on many Colorado trips.
—Laurence Parent

Right: Picture-perfect at any time of year, the Maroon Bells pose with a sun-kissed blush above Maroon Lake. The twin Fourteeners Maroon Peak and North Maroon Peak draw thousands of visitors every year. LAURENCE PARENT

Title page: Yankee Boy Basin's renowned wildflower display seems to dance through the meadows of the Uncompahgre National Forest. LAURENCE PARENT

Front cover: The rainbow colors of autumn brighten the foothills of the San Juan Mountains. BLAINE HARRINGTON III

Back cover: Red rock spires reach skyward in the Garden of the Gods outside of Colorado Springs. LAURENCE PARENT

ISBN: 978-1-56037-637-8

© 2016 by Farcountry Press
Photography © 2016 by Blaine Harrington III and Laurence Parent

For more information about our books, write Farcountry Press, P.O. Box 5630, Helena, MT 59604; call (800) 821-3874; or visit www.farcountrypress.com.

Produced in the United States of America.
Printed in China.

20 19 18 17 16   1 2 3 4 5

Above: Wildflowers of every hue, including the white-and-lavender columbine, Colorado's state flower, brighten a mountain meadow in Yankee Boy Basin near Ridgway. LAURENCE PARENT

Left: Hikers pause near the summit of 14,005-foot Mount of the Holy Cross. Colorado is home to many "Fourteeners," peaks that reach at least 14,000 feet in elevation—54 of them in total, though differences in the definition of "peak" put that count at between 52 and 56. LAURENCE PARENT

Far right: The sophisticated Stanley Hotel was opened in 1909 by Freelan Oscar Stanley, the inventor of the Stanley Steamer automobile, to entertain high society tourists from the east. The hotel overlooks Estes Park and the peaks of Rocky Mountain National Park. LAURENCE PARENT

Right: This bronze statue of a World War II-era ski trooper in Vail commemorates the brave service of the Army's Tenth Mountain Division, which trained at Fort Hale near Vail. BLAINE HARRINGTON III

Below: After a day on the ski slopes at Breckenridge, Keystone, or Copper Mountain, Christmastime visitors to Frisco can enjoy the charming shops and restaurants, along with a cheery display of holiday lights. LAURENCE PARENT

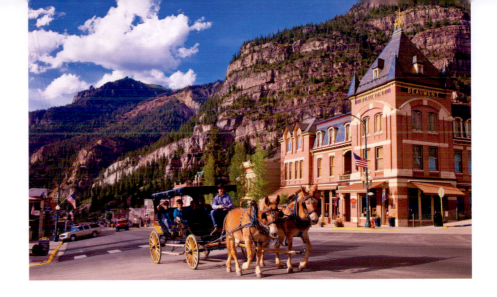

Above, top: Ringed by the dramatic peaks of the San Juan Mountains in southwestern Colorado, the historic mining town of Ouray is known as the Switzerland of America. BLAINE HARRINGTON III

Above, bottom: Hovenweep National Monument preserves six Ancestral Puebloan communities skillfully constructed between 1200 and 1300 A.D. The tower of the Holly Group, along with nearby sites Horseshoe, Hackberry, and Cutthroat Castle, stand within Canyons of the Ancients National Monument. LAURENCE PARENT

Left: Picturesque Willow Lake lies at about 11,600 feet near Crestone in the Sangre de Cristo Mountains. Dubbed "Blood of Christ" by Spanish explorers, this mountain range in the southern Rockies includes nine peaks rising at least 14,000 feet in elevation. LAURENCE PARENT

Facing page: The gondola between Telluride and Mountain Village is a one-of-a-kind transport, providing a scenic ride to the slopes for skiers and snowboarders and free public transportation for others. BLAINE HARRINGTON III

Right: The Coors Brewery in Golden is one of the largest brewing sites in the world, and its popular tours even include a beer tasting. Adolph Coors, a Prussian immigrant, founded the brewery in 1873. BLAINE HARRINGTON III

Below: A budding bronco rider holds tight to a sheep during a "mutton busting" rodeo event. BLAINE HARRINGTON III

Facing page: The dramatic red sandstone formations of the Garden of the Gods in Colorado Springs are formed from the eroded debris of ancient mountains known as the Ancestral Rockies. Rock-climbing, hiking, horseback riding, and road biking are popular activities in this awe-inspiring city park. BLAINE HARRINGTON III

Left: For more than 30 years, the Telluride Balloon Festival has attracted visitors from all over the world to witness the flight of brilliantly colored hot air balloons across the Telluride Valley. Volunteers can help inflate the balloons and, perhaps, ride up, up, and away with one. BLAINE HARRINGTON III

Below: Built in 1882 to haul gold and silver ore from southwest Colorado's San Juan Mountains, today the Durango & Silverton Narrow Gauge Railroad carries passengers through 45 miles of gorgeous scenery. LAURENCE PARENT

Far left: The high mountains of the Front, Sawatch, and Mosquito Ranges ring the valley of South Park, and historic mining towns Fairplay, Alma, Como, and Jefferson dot the valley floor. LAURENCE PARENT

Left: The Pikes Peak Cog Railway carries visitors year-round from Manitou Springs to the 14,110-foot summit of Pikes Peak, along grades as steep as 24 degrees. Pikes Peak is billed as "America's Mountain," and the view from the top inspired Katharine Lee Bates to pen "America the Beautiful" in 1893. BLAINE HARRINGTON III

Below: Through most the year, groups of Rocky Mountain bighorn sheep, Colorado's state animal, live in separate groups—the rams in "bachelor herds" and the ewes and lambs, like these on Mount Evans, in "nursery herds." In late fall, both groups gather for the rut, when the rams battle head-to-head for mates. LAURENCE PARENT

Above: The hip city of Boulder is known not only as the home of the University of Colorado, but also as a thriving center of alternative culture. The pedestrian-only Pearl Street Mall, full of restaurants, shops, street performers, fountains, and sculptures, is a great place for people-watching.
COURTESY OF DOWNTOWN BOULDER (DBI.ORG)

Right: Snowmass Village offers visitors a quiet stay and endless opportunities for hiking, biking, and skiing. Snowmass Ski Resort has the most vertical feet of skiing of any resort in the United States, and there is easy access to nearby Aspen Mountain, Aspen Highlands, and Buttermilk ski areas.
LAURENCE PARENT

Facing page: The 750-foot-high dunes of Great Sand Dunes National Park and Preserve are the tallest in North America. Visitors can sandboard, sand sled, play on the beach along Medano Creek, hike, camp, picnic, or simply savor the pristine beauty of the shifting sands.
LAURENCE PARENT

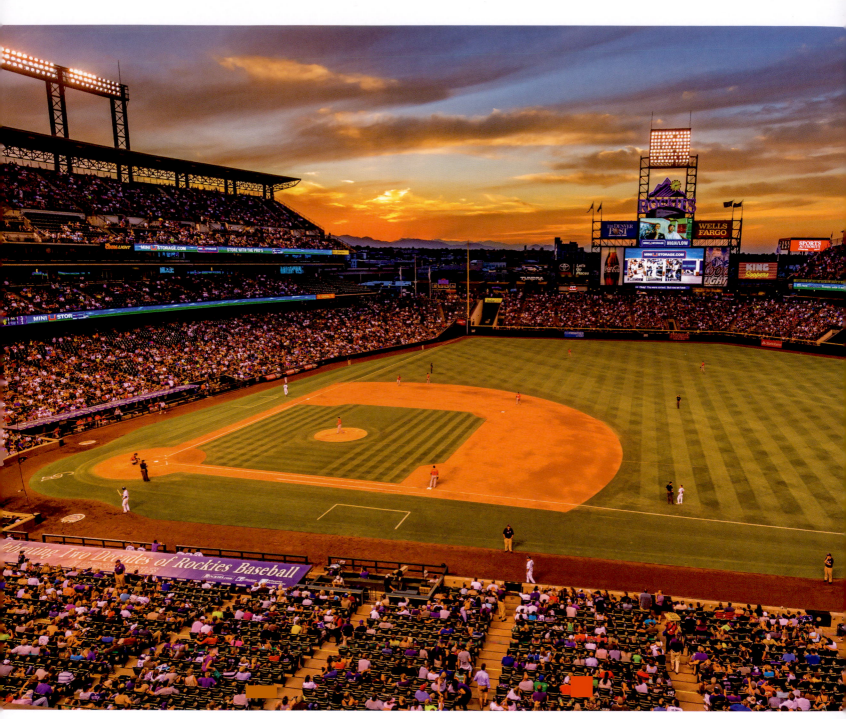

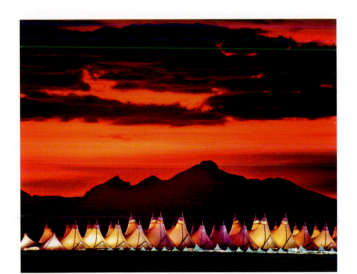

Far left: Coors Field is the home of the Colorado Rockies, a Major League Baseball team. While most of its seats are green, those on the 20th row are purple, commemorating their location at 5,280 feet above sea level in the Mile High City of Denver. BLAINE HARRINGTON III

Left: Covering 54 square miles, Denver International Airport is the largest airport in the United States by total land area. The Jeppesen Terminal's peaked roof evokes the mountains to the west, as well as tepees used by Plains Indians. BLAINE HARRINGTON III

Below: The unique glass, steel, and aluminum architecture of the Air Force Academy's Cadet Chapel mirrors the dramatic peaks of the Rocky Mountains rising just to the West. The academy, just north of Colorado Springs, prepares its 4,000 cadets for careers as officers in the United States Air Force. BLAINE HARRINGTON III

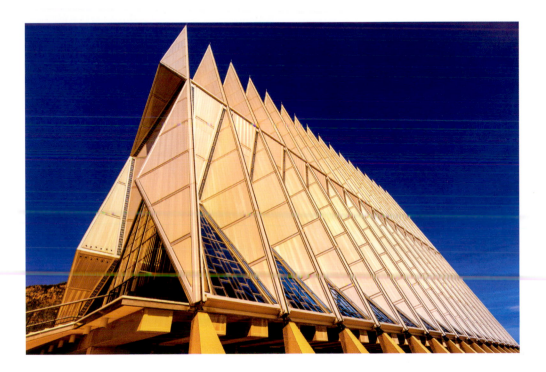

Facing page: In mid-summer, the surface of Nymph Lake in Rocky Mountain National Park is often covered with lily pads. LAURENCE PARENT

Right: The snow-covered slopes of the Mummy Range rise above Trail Ridge Road in Rocky Mountain National Park. The road is among the highest continuous paved roads in the United States, traversing 48 miles between Estes Park and Grand Lake and reaching 12,183 feet in elevation. LAURENCE PARENT

Below: In summer, Rocky Mountain elk move up onto the grassy landscape of the alpine tundra above timberline to graze. A mature bull elk weighs around 700 pounds. LAURENCE PARENT

Facing page: Another sunset finds the face of Balcony House. Ancestral Puebloans, the ancestors of present-day Pueblo peoples, built and occupied the complex cliff dwellings at Mesa Verde National Park from about 1190 to 1300 A.D. LAURENCE PARENT

Left: A dramatic 17.1-mile jeep road traverses 13,114-foot Imogene Pass from Telluride to Ouray in the San Juan Mountains. BLAINE HARRINGTON III

Below: What's around the next bend? Forest roads, including this one through an aspen grove in the San Isabel National Forest in Huerfano County, can lead intrepid drivers, cyclists, and other explorers through journeys of discovery in the mountains. LAURENCE PARENT

Above: In autumn, the golden leaves of aspen trees highlight the vibrant buildings of Silverton. BLAINE HARRINGTON III

Right: The Royal Gorge Bridge near Cañon City carries travelers across the plunging gorge 956 feet above the pounding waters of the Arkansas River. It is the highest bridge in the United States. PHOTO BY EVE NAGODE, COURTESY OF ROYAL GORGE BRIDGE

Facing page: Fed by numerous waterfalls, the iridescent waters of Glenwood Canyon's Hanging Lake glow with unearthly colors caused by dissolved minerals. The hike to this alluring lake, a National Natural Landmark, is one of the most popular in the state. BLAINE HARRINGTON III

Facing page: A rainbow of summer flowers highlights Civic Center Park and the 24-karat gold dome of the Colorado State Capitol in Denver. A marker on the capitol's 13th step marks one mile above sea level. BLAINE HARRINGTON III

Left: May through October, Elitch Gardens Theme and Water Park in downtown Denver hums with activity and dozens of rides and attractions, from sedate to thrilling. BLAINE HARRINGTON III

Below: Thousands of lights illuminate the Denver Botanic Gardens during the holiday season's Blossoms of Light display. BLAINE HARRINGTON III

Above: A hiker traverses the Keyhole along the trail to the summit of 14,259-foot Longs Peak in Rocky Mountain National Park, a challenging 15-mile round trip that may require 10 to 15 hours of hiking and climbing. LAURENCE PARENT

Right: The Gunnison River carves a tortuous route through the towering granite cliffs of Black Canyon of the Gunnison National Park, near Montrose. Over two million years, the river, wind, and weather have carved this dramatic gorge, which reaches a depth of 2,722 feet. LAURENCE PARENT

Above: Snowboarders and skiers find abundant challenges at Colorado's world-class terrain parks. BLAINE HARRINGTON III

Right: Snowmass Village's Rim Trail offers hiking and mountain biking for all skill levels. BLAINE HARRINGTON III

Facing page: Just on the outskirts of Grand Junction, Colorado National Monument's red rock canyons and soaring monoliths make it a great place for hiking, climbing, and wildlife watching. LAURENCE PARENT

Above: The sleek California Zephyr train stops at Union Station in downtown Denver en route from San Francisco to Chicago. Built in 1881 and reopened in 2014 following a major renovation, elegant Union Station is a bustling site for sightseeing, dining, and nightlife. BLAINE HARRINGTON III

Right: In fall, the golden leaves of aspen trees blanket the lower slopes of 11,814-foot Ophir Pass in the San Juan Mountains near Silverton. This popular four-wheel-drive road overlooks the remains of the Ophir Loop railroad trestle and mining town of Ophir. BLAINE HARRINGTON III

Far right: A quintessential Rocky Mountain sunset highlights the skyline of downtown Denver. BLAINE HARRINGTON III

Above: The distinctive, boxy summit of Longs Peak marks the horizon along Trail Ridge Road in Rocky Mountain National Park. Longs is the only Fourteener in the park.
LAURENCE PARENT

Left: Ptarmigan Lake in the Sawatch Range is a popular place for both hikers and anglers. Colorado offers many options for fishing—it boasts 6,000 miles of streams, 2,000 lakes, and 35 species of fish.
LAURENCE PARENT

Far left: Mills Lake in Rocky Mountain National Park lies in a bowl below the jagged, saw like ridge known as Keyboard of the Winds.
LAURENCE PARENT

Above: The flags of four states (Colorado, Arizona, Utah, and New Mexico) and three nations (the United States, the Navajo Nation, and the Ute Mountain Ute Tribe) mark Four Corners Monument, the only place in the United States where four states meet. LAURENCE PARENT

Right: Two thousand yogis practice together at Yoga On the Rocks in Red Rocks Amphitheater, Morrison. The stunning outdoor venue, nestled among dramatic red sandstone formations, is also a popular concert and event site. BLAINE HARRINGTON III

Far right: A twisted juniper marks the breathtaking vista along the rim of the Black Canyon of the Gunnison at Dragon Point, near Montrose. LAURENCE PARENT

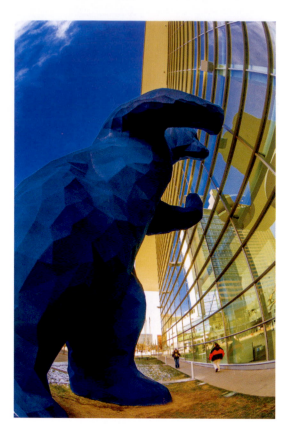

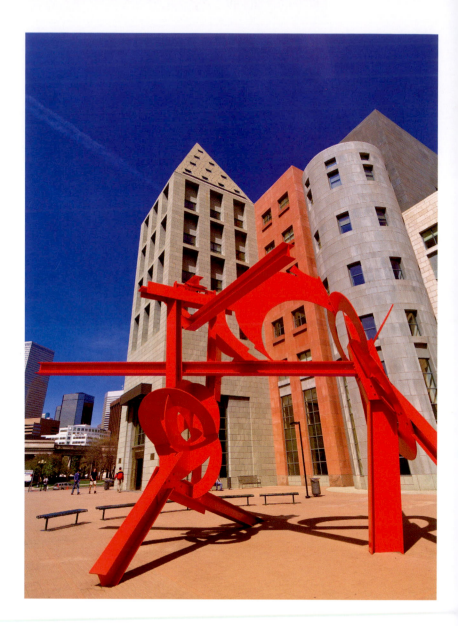

Above: Popularly known as the Big Blue Bear, the 40-foot-tall fiberglass and steel sculpture *I See What You Mean,* by Lawrence Argent, peers in the windows at the Colorado Convention Center in downtown Denver. BLAINE HARRINGTON III

Right: The plaza between the Denver Art Museum and the Denver Public Library displays Mark di Suvero's *Lao Tzu,* a 16-ton abstract steel sculpture that doubles as an irresistible climbing structure for kids. BLAINE HARRINGTON III

Facing page: Sixteenth Street Mall, a tree-lined, pedestrian promenade covering 1.25 miles in downtown Denver, is a major tourist destination with shops, dining, street performers, and historical attractions. Footsore visitors can ride the free mall shuttle. BLAINE HARRINGTON III

39

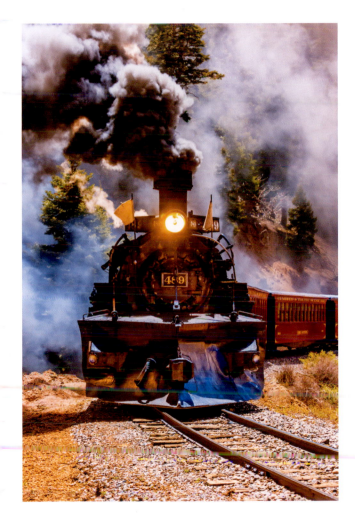

Facing page: Evening shadows fill a valley below the Continental Divide near Cottonwood Pass. LAURENCE PARENT

Left: Cinders and smoke flying, a steam locomotive charges along the Cumbres & Toltec Scenic Railroad. This old-time railroading experience carries riders 64 miles through the southern Rockies between Chama, New Mexico, and Antonito, Colorado. BLAINE HARRINGTON III

Below: Ancient rock art, caves, canyons, and hoodoos mark Picture Canyon, part of Comanche National Grassland in the far southeast reaches of Colorado. COURTESY OF UNITED STATES FOREST SERVICE

Far right: The granite column of the Curecanti Needle rises 700 feet above Morrow Point Reservoir in Black Canyon of the Gunnison National Park. LAURENCE PARENT

Right: Locals and visitors flock to micro-breweries across Colorado for good beer and good company, and the rooftop bar of the Ouray Brewing Company is no exception. The town of Ouray is named for Chief Ouray, who is honored for his efforts to keep peace between settlers and Ute Indians. BLAINE HARRINGTON III

Below: The vibrant storefronts of the historic town of Silverton resemble the set of a Western movie. Silverton, the northern terminus of the Durango & Silverton Narrow Gauge Railroad, had its heyday between 1874 and the early 1900s, when area mines produced tons of gold and silver. LAURENCE PARENT

Above: Rafters on the Yampa River float past Tiger Wall in Dinosaur National Monument, a perfect escape for paleontology enthusiasts and adventurers alike. COURTESY OF NATIONAL PARK SERVICE

Left: Horses in a snowy pasture along Owl Creek, near Aspen, evoke Colorado's ranching heritage. LAURENCE PARENT

Facing page: About 700 years ago, volcanic rock slid down the mountain and blocked the Lake Fork Gunnison River. This event, known as the Slumgullion Slide, created Lake San Cristobal, Colorado's second-largest natural lake and the namesake of nearby Lake City. LAURENCE PARENT

Above: In recent years, Amish families have joined longtime Colorado ranch families in cultivating the fertile land of the Wet Mountain and San Luis valleys. LAURENCE PARENT

Right: Representing the ranching heritage of Colorado, the bronze sculpture *Scottish Angus Cow and Calf,* by Dan Ostermiller, stands outside the Frederic C. Hamilton Building of the Denver Art Museum. The massive calf stands ten feet tall, and its mother three feet taller. BLAINE HARRINGTON III

Facing page: The Millennium Bridge, which connects downtown Denver's 16th Street Mall with Riverfront Park, resembles the mast of a great ship. Visitors can ascend stairs or take an elevator to the deck for great views of downtown and across the South Platte River. BLAINE HARRINGTON III

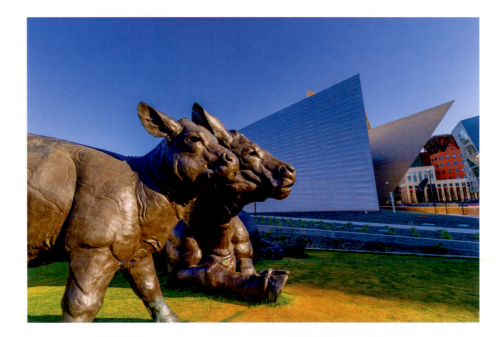

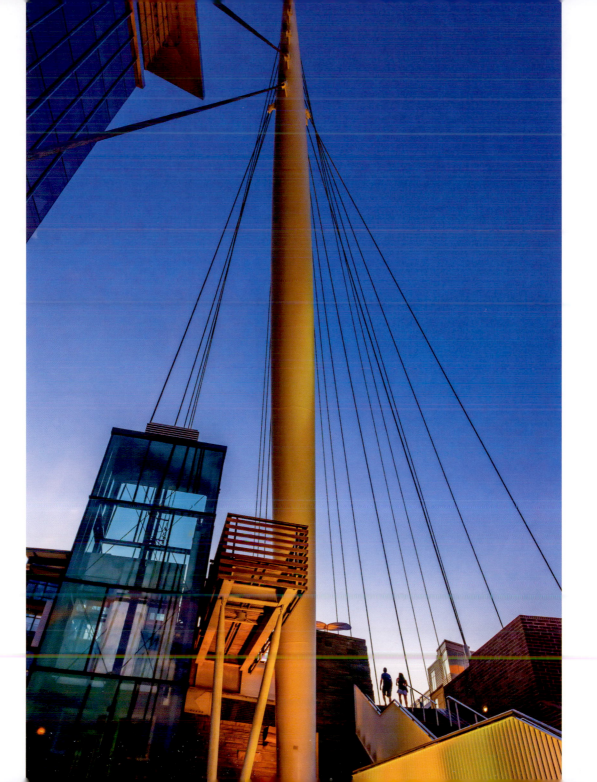

Above: Snow blankets the ground and flecks the green-needled limbs of ponderosa pine trees in a montane forest in Rocky Mountain National Park. LAURENCE PARENT

Left: Hardy glacier lilies bloom next to a summer snow bank in the Indian Peaks Wilderness. LAURENCE PARENT

Facing page: Near Nathrop, hikers traverse a subalpine meadow on the trail to Ptarmigan Lake, named for the grouse-like birds that live at and above the timberline. Ptarmigan are camouflaged a mottled brown in summer, then turn white with the winter snow. LAURENCE PARENT

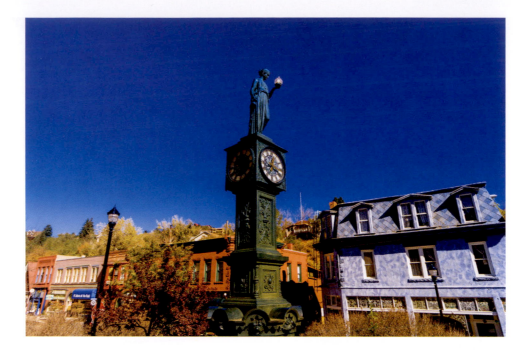

Above: In the shadow of Pikes Peak, the natural mineral springs of Manitou Springs have long attracted visitors, from generations of Native Americans to modern tourists. This charming town's scenic beauty and clear mountain air complete the experience. BLAINE HARRINGTON III

Right: Stalactites seem to drip from the ceiling of a cave at Glenwood Caverns Adventure Park. Mineral-rich water trickling from the cave ceiling creates stalactites and their upside-down cousins, stalagmites. BLAINE HARRINGTON III

Far right: Hikers descend the summit of Redcloud Peak and cross the saddle to the top of Sunshine Peak—two Fourteeners in one hike. To qualify as a separate peak, each summit must rise at least 300 feet above any connecting ridge.
LAURENCE PARENT

Above: Not for the faint of heart, the Giant Canyon Swing swoops thrill-seekers 1,300 feet above the Colorado River at Glenwood Caverns Adventure Park in Glenwood Springs. BLAINE HARRINGTON III

Left: The trail to 14,309-foot Uncompahgre Peak, in the Uncompahgre Wilderness of southwestern Colorado, showcases the dramatic, treeless terrain of Colorado's high alpine tundra. Wetterhorn Peak (14,015 feet) is visible in the distance. LAURENCE PARENT

Above: The remaining buildings of Ashcroft, a former silver mining town, slumber beneath the snow. The rise and fall of industries such as mining, rail, and agriculture created as many as 1,500 ghost towns across Colorado. LAURENCE PARENT

Right: Highly adaptable red foxes are common neighbors in the parks and open spaces of Colorado's cities. BLAINE HARRINGTON III

Far right: Snow creates a mystical landscape along the Roaring Fork River, which flows through the North Star Nature Preserve near Aspen. LAURENCE PARENT

Above: Switchbacks carve a route down from Black Bear Pass, a jeep trail over the San Juan Mountains above Telluride. BLAINE HARRINGTON III

Left: A calm pond along Paradise Divide, near Crested Butte, mirrors the spectacular scenery of the high mountains. BLAINE HARRINGTON III

Above: Although Colorado's downhill skiing and snowboarding facilities get more attention, its snows are perfect for enjoying other winter sports such as snowshoeing and cross-country skiing. The skiers above take advantage of the Frisco Nordic Center in Summit County. LAURENCE PARENT

Right: The reflections of two Colorado Fourteeners—14,034-foot Redcloud Peak and 14,001-foot Sunshine Peak—decorate the quiet surface of a beaver pond on the Lake Fork Gunnison River. LAURENCE PARENT

Above: A crisp autumn day in Crested Butte beckons visitors to the charming shops and restaurants along Elk Avenue. Crested Butte is a hiking and mountain biking mecca in summer, and an outstanding ski resort in winter. LAURENCE PARENT

Left: A waterfall crashes through the narrow opening of Devil's Punchbowl along the Roaring Fork River. Tucked away in the mountains near Aspen, this area of rock grottoes and ice caves is easily accessible from Independence Pass. LAURENCE PARENT

Right: This stretch of U.S. Route 550, dubbed the Million Dollar Highway, traverses 25 miles through the Uncompahgre Gorge and Red Mountain Pass between Ouray and Silverton. The nickname may refer to the cost to build this challenging road, or to speculation that the roadbed holds valuable ore in this historic gold and silver mining region. BLAINE HARRINGTON III

Facing page: Early morning mist shrouds the town of Crested Butte as the aspens on surrounding mountainsides flame to gold in the dawn light. Crested Butte transformed its economy as mining declined, and is now a major summer and winter tourism destination. LAURENCE PARENT

Above: A rodeo queen proudly carries the Stars and Stripes at the Snowmass Rodeo, held once a week throughout the summer at Snowmass Village. These high-adrenaline events test skills of horsemanship and roping that have long been valuable in ranching. BLAINE HARRINGTON III

Right: Snowboarders and skiers of all abilities will find runs, jumps, rails, half pipes, and wild terrain at Colorado's famous ski slopes. BLAINE HARRINGTON III

Far right: The ancient cliff dwellings of Spruce Tree House in Mesa Verde National Park glow in special evening lighting. Ancestral Puebloans built the community between 1211 and 1278 A.D., and it contains 130 rooms and eight kivas, or ceremonial chambers. The park contains more than 4,000 archeological sites, both under the cliffs and atop the mesa. BLAINE HARRINGTON III

Above: North Clear Creek Falls, visible from the Silverthread Scenic Byway near Creede, plunges about 100 feet into the creek below. LAURENCE PARENT

Left: The dunes of Great Sand Dunes National Park and Preserve are constantly reshaped by the wind before the air currents pass up and over the Sangre de Cristo Mountains. LAURENCE PARENT

The ever-growing skyline of downtown Denver stretches from the golden-domed Colorado State Capitol to the lighted City and County Building on the left. The Greek-style amphitheater of Civic Center Park, built during the City Beautiful movement of the early 20th century, graces the left foreground. BLAINE HARRINGTON III

Facing page: A hiker takes the last few steps to the summit of 14,003-foot Huron Peak, which rewards climbers with a view of the breathtaking mountains of the Sawatch Range. This mountain range has 15 peaks rising above 14,000 feet. LAURENCE PARENT

Right: Summer visitors enjoy bumper boats on the pond at Copper Mountain, conveniently located along Interstate 70 west of Denver. Copper Mountain is both a bustling winter ski resort and a popular summertime retreat. BLAINE HARRINGTON III

Below: The holiday spirit is on full display as lights brighten the charming storefronts and sidewalks of historic Old Town Littleton. BLAINE HARRINGTON III

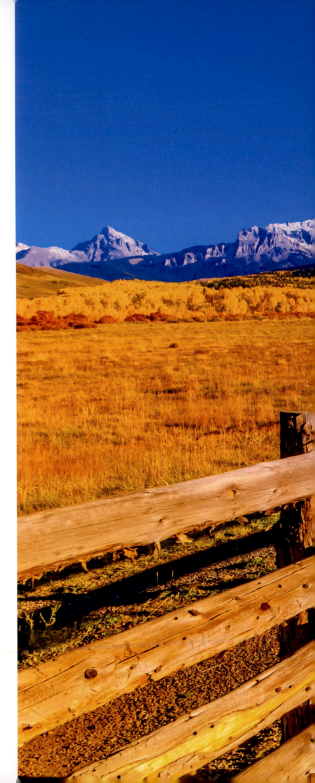

Above: The Rio Grande originates in the San Juan Mountains and meanders through this valley above Creede on its way to New Mexico. Its waters travel nearly 2,000 miles to empty into the Gulf of Mexico near Brownsville, Texas. LAURENCE PARENT

Right: A log fence marks the boundaries of the Last Dollar Ranch, resting in the shadow of the Sneffels Range between Ridgway and Telluride. BLAINE HARRINGTON III

Above: "Independence Eve" fireworks light up the sky over Denver's City and County Building on July 3. The building is decorated with colorful lights for Independence Day and for the holiday season. BLAINE HARRINGTON III

Right: Since 1888, guests have flocked to the Glenwood Hot Springs Pool, the largest of its kind in the world, for a therapeutic cure or just to enjoy a warm soak. BLAINE HARRINGTON III

Facing page: Kayakers traverse a bend in the Colorado River below the striking walls of Glenwood Canyon, just east of Glenwood Springs. BLAINE HARRINGTON III

Above: Coopersmith's Pub & Brewing has been a popular fixture on Old Town Square in downtown Fort Collins for two decades. The idyllic Old Town neighborhood, lined with shops and restaurants, was the model for much of Disneyland's Main Street, U.S.A. COURTESY OF VISIT FORT COLLINS

Right: Fall colors blaze on the lower slopes of the Sneffels Range in the San Juan Mountains. BLAINE HARRINGTON III

Far right: Clouds shroud the high peaks of Rocky Mountain National Park. BLAINE HARRINGTON III

Right: The Leadville, Colorado & Southern Railroad carries visitors on a 2.5-hour scenic ride through the forests, mountains, and colorful history of the central Rockies. LAURENCE PARENT

Below: Near Buena Vista, tunnels blasted through rock remain as evidence of the one-time route of the Colorado Midland Railroad, now the Old Colorado Midland Grade Road. LAURENCE PARENT

BLAINE HARRINGTON III has traveled the world for the last 40 years, working on assignment for major news, travel, business, and inflight magazines in the U.S. and abroad. He has photographed parts of a number of books for National Geographic, Time-Life Books, and other coffee table books and travel guidebooks, including more than 60 Insight Guides. A Colorado native, Harrington left in 1973 to attend Brooks Institute of Photography in California. He then worked in fashion, advertising, and editorial photography in New York, Paris, Amsterdam, and Zurich. Harrington was named Travel Photographer of the Year by the Society of American Travel Writers in 2005 and 2006. He returned to Colorado in 1995 and uses Denver as his home base. He has participated in many of the exciting things he's photographed, including Pamplona's Running of the Bulls, ski mountaineering the Haute Route in the Alps, and bungee jumping in South Africa and New Zealand. His goal for life: go everywhere, meet everyone, try everything! See more of Harrington's work at BlaineHarrington.com.

LAURENCE PARENT was born and raised in New Mexico. After receiving a petroleum engineering degree at the University of Texas at Austin in 1981, he practiced engineering for six years before becoming a full-time freelance photographer and writer specializing in landscape, travel, and nature subjects. He was drawn to the profession by a love of the outdoors and a desire to work for himself. He specializes in 4x5 film and digital landscapes and outdoor sports images, and has stock from almost every state and Canadian province, and several countries. Parent has published 42 books, including several from Farcountry Press, and his photos appear in many calendars. He contributes regularly to regional publications in New Mexico and Texas. Other work includes posters, advertising, museum exhibits, postcards, and brochures. He makes his home in the Austin, Texas, area with his wife Patricia and two children. For more of Parent's photography, visit LaurenceParent.com.